IN FOCUS: NATIVE AMERICANS

CHEROKEE
HISTORY AND CULTURE

MARK STEWART

Published in 2026 by Cavendish Square Publishing, LLC
2544 Clinton Street, Buffalo, NY 14224

Copyright © 2026 by Cavendish Square Publishing, LLC

No part of this publication may be reproduced, stored in a retrieval system, or transmitted in any form or by any means—electronic, mechanical, photocopying, recording, or otherwise—without the prior permission of the copyright owner. Request for permission should be addressed to Permissions, Cavendish Square Publishing, 2544 Clinton Street, Buffalo, NY 14224. Tel (877) 980-4450; fax (877) 980-4454.

Website: cavendishsq.com

This publication represents the opinions and views of the author based on his or her personal experience, knowledge, and research. The information in this book serves as a general guide only. The author and publisher have used their best efforts in preparing this book and disclaim liability rising directly or indirectly from the use and application of this book.

Portions of this work were originally authored by Cassandra Zardes and published as *Cherokee* (Spotlight on Native Americans). All new material in this edition authored by Mark Stewart.

The website addresses (URLs) included in this book were valid at the time of going to press. However, it is possible that contents or addresses may have changed since the publication of this book. No responsibility for any such changes can be accepted by either the author or the publisher.

Publisher: Katie Kawa
Book Design: Lisa Miley

Portions of this work were reviewed by: Robert J. Conley, Former Sequoyah Distinguished Professor at Western Carolina University and Director of Native American Studies at Morningside College and Montana State University.

Special thanks to the Oklahoma Historical Society.

Dennis Flaherty (4); Henry Timberlake (5*); George Caleb Bingham/Bridgeman Art Library (6*); Oklahoma Historical Society (7); John Berkey / Getty Images (9); National Park Service (10*); Charles Ferdinand Wimar (11*); George Catlin/National Gallery of Art (12*); Charles Bird King (13*); Carlisle Indian School Digital Resource Center (14); Native Stock (16, 18, 27, 24); Georgia Tribe of Eastern Cherokee (17*); Author's Collection (19, 22); Cherokee Nation/Cherokee National Holiday (20, 24); Library of Congress (21*); Internet archive (23), Sogospleman (25); Ken Rahaim/ National Museum of the American Indian (26); Carol Highsmith/Library of Congress (28).

Cover images (clockwise from top): Oklahoma Historical Society; Carol Highsmith/Library of Congress*; De Lancey Gill/Smithsonian Institution National Anthropological Archives*; Native Stock; Henry Inman/National Portrait Gallery*; Native Stock.

*These images are in the public domain.

Cataloging-in-Publication Data
Names: Stewart, Mark, 1960 July 7-.
Title: Cherokee history and culture / Mark Stewart.
Description: Buffalo, NY : Cavendish Square Publishing, 2026. | Series: In focus: Native Americans | Includes glossary and index.
Identifiers: ISBN 9781502674975 (pbk.) | ISBN 9781502674982 (library bound) | ISBN 9781502674999 (ebook)
Subjects: LCSH: Cherokee Indians--Juvenile literature. | Cherokee Indians--History--Juvenile literature.
Classification: LCC E99.C5 S94 2026 | DDC 975.004'97557--dc23

CPSIA compliance information: Batch #CS26CSQ: For further information contact Cavendish Square Publishing LLC at 1-877-980-4450.
Printed in the United States of America

CONTENTS

I AM THE LAND 4

FIRST CONTACT 8

I AM A WARRIOR 10

A NEW REALITY 14

BEING CHEROKEE 16

SOMETHING SACRED 20

PAST, PRESENT, FUTURE 24

GLOSSARY AND FURTHER READING 30

ABOUT THE AUTHOR 31

INDEX 32

ABOUT OUR GLOSSARY

In this book, there may be several words or terms you are reading for the first time, or words that are familiar but used in an unusual way. All of these words appear in **bold type** throughout the book and are defined on page 30.

I AM THE LAND

The Appalachian Mountains stretch over 2,000 miles (3,218 km) from Central Alabama into Eastern Canada. The southern portion of the Appalachians touches the states of Kentucky, West Virginia, Virginia, North Carolina, South Carolina, Georgia, Tennessee, and Alabama. It is a diverse landscape that includes high cliffs and rock outcrops, huge granite **domes**, fast-moving rivers and streams, and an **ecosystem** that supports an amazing number of plant and animal species. For hundreds of

This illustration shows three Cherokee leaders who visited London, England, in 1762.

years, the Cherokee people lived in this region, hunting in the forests and farming the valleys. Their territory formed a natural barrier between the coastal regions to the east and the interior to the west. Control over the Southern Appalachians gave them great power and influence.

The Cherokees were not the first people to live in this part of North America. Evidence of human habitation

◀ The Cherokee people made the Southern Appalachian Mountains their home more than five centuries ago.

This painting shows frontiersman Daniel Boone leading settlers west through the Cumberland Gap in Cherokee territory.

dates back at least 12,000 years. The Cherokees moved into this vast region sometime before 1500. Because their language has similarities to the languages spoken by the Iroquois, historians believe they may have migrated south from the Great Lakes region. They have historical links to the ancient, mound-building Mississippian culture, too.

The Cherokee people used a deep knowledge of their world to blend the skills of hunter-gatherer and agricultural societies. Understanding the seasonal movement of large game and the cycles of plants for food and medicine guaranteed that Cherokee towns and villages would not have to rely entirely on farming. However, it was the crops they grew—including the "Three Sisters" of corn, beans, and squash—that enabled them to thrive even during lean times.

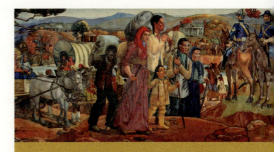

The **resilience** and flexibility of Cherokee culture also extended to their political skills. In the early 1800s, when it became clear that the United States government **coveted** their land, Cherokee leaders convinced their people to align their lifestyle, economy, and customs with those of the Americans. They adopted Christianity, operated **plantations**, and educated their children in American schools. They learned U.S. laws and used them to protect their rights.

More so than any other North American tribe, the Cherokees tried to find common ground between Native and European cultures and live in harmony without losing their land. In the end, this effort was not successful. It ended with an episode of **ethnic cleansing** that came to be known as the "Trail of Tears."

FIRST CONTACT

The first recorded contact between Europeans and the Cherokee people occurred in 1540. Spanish explorer Hernando de Soto found the "Cheloque" to be friendly and they made an agreement allowing Spain to conduct mining and **smelting** operations in a portion of their territory. In 1670, England established the colony of South Carolina and soon involved the Cherokees and other tribes in the trading of enslaved people. Multiple conflicts between the Indigenous people and the colonists followed, as well as raiding and warfare between neighboring tribes. For example, the Cherokee and Creek (Muscogee) people fought on and off for 50 years.

In 1738, a **smallpox** epidemic broke out in some Cherokee villages. By the end of 1739, half the tribe had died. This included survivors who took their own lives because of the **disfiguring** effects of the disease. This not only reduced Cherokee political power, it also made the people question the power of their religious leaders and ceremonies.

This painting shows an early encounter between Spanish explorers and members of the Cherokee and Creek people.

During the American Revolution, the Cherokees sided with the British and began raiding settlements on their land. The colonists retaliated by burning more than 50 Cherokee towns and selling their captives into slavery. Cherokee leaders convinced their people to work with the Americans in the years that followed, but it did little more than delay their **resettlement** and removal.

I AM A WARRIOR

Traditional Cherokee tribal leaders included a white chief and a red chief. The white chief handled matters of politics and peace, while the red chief was in charge of forming war parties. Cherokee warriors were trained to protect their towns and villages, and respond to raiding parties that entered their territory. They were effective raiders themselves—moving swiftly and silently over great distances to attack rival tribes and settlers along the **frontier**.

Cherokee warriors were heavily tattooed. Many of their markings signified achievements in combat. They pierced their skin

◀ This illustration shows Oconostota, a great Cherokee war chief of the mid-1700s.

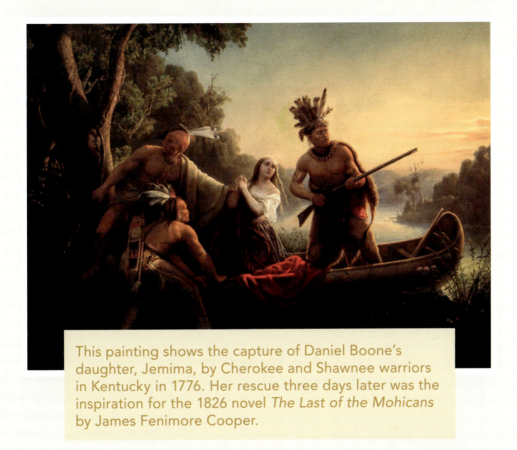

This painting shows the capture of Daniel Boone's daughter, Jemima, by Cherokee and Shawnee warriors in Kentucky in 1776. Her rescue three days later was the inspiration for the 1826 novel *The Last of the Mohicans* by James Fenimore Cooper.

with sharp animal bones and rubbed charcoal or colored plants into the wounds. The patterns of dots formed symbolic designs. Many warriors wore colorful cloth **turbans** decorated with bright feathers. These were also worn at important ceremonies and political meetings.

The vast majority of Cherokee fighters were men, but female warriors were not unheard of. The word for these women was *ghigau*. It meant "war woman." The term was also used to honor someone who had done

This painting of two Cherokee chiefs shows one with a peace pipe and another with a rifle.

something of great importance within the community. In this context, it meant "beloved woman."

The Cherokees fought on foot. In close combat, they used oversized knives, tomahawks, and war clubs. War clubs were made from tree roots that featured a heavy ball on one end. Tomahawks, which doubled as chopping tools, could be thrown with great accuracy by Cherokee warriors. The knife favored by the Cherokee warrior was often a foot long and sharpened on only one side. It later became known as the Bowie knife after soldier and frontiersman Jim Bowie made some slight changes to its design. Although Cherokee warriors became skilled marksmen after acquiring European firearms, many still preferred to use the bow and arrow. A favorite wood for bow-making came from the black locust tree.

Cherokee warriors fought on the side of the British during the **French and Indian War**, and again during the American Revolution. They joined General Andrew Jackson in America's military action against the Creeks in 1813–14. Cherokee and Creek warriors knew each other well from decades of conflict. Jackson—who would later become the architect of Indian Removal as U.S. president—depended heavily on the speed and skill of Cherokees in important battles.

General Andrew Jackson insisted that his Cherokee allies wear white feathers or deer tails in their hair so his troops would recognize them quickly during the fighting and not attack them by mistake.

A NEW REALITY

In 1830, the United States passed the Indian Removal Act. It gave the government the right to resettle tribes in western territories. President Andrew Jackson, who had witnessed violence between settlers and Native Americans firsthand as a young man—and had an adopted son who was born into the Creek tribe—

believed that Indigenous people would perish if they were not moved out of harm's way.

Of course, there were other reasons for the law. One year earlier, gold was discovered on Cherokee land in the mountains north of Atlanta, Georgia. A "gold rush" started and the state demanded that the **federal** government move the tribe out of this valuable land. In 1835, a Cherokee leader signed the Treaty of New Echota, which agreed to the terms of removal. He only represented a small portion of the Cherokee people. However, in 1838 the government used this document to force the entire tribe off its lands.

The U.S. Army divided 16,000 Cherokees into thirteen groups with a plan to move them west to Oklahoma. Delays, drought, poor supplies, mismanagement, and harsh winter weather killed a quarter of the people. More died of illnesses after reaching their destination. Their journey became known as the Trail of Tears.

◀ During the 1800s, many Native American children were sent to government-run boarding schools that forced them to abandon their culture. This 1895 photo shows a group of Cherokee students at the Carlisle Indian School in Pennsylvania.

BEING CHEROKEE

The traditional Cherokee lifestyle was based on farming. The Southern Appalachian valleys where they lived were fed by rivers and streams, and the soil was fertile enough to grow a variety of crops that could be eaten fresh or stored for the winter. Crops grown on town farm plots were tended by everyone and belonged to everyone. Additionally, each family worked its own fields.

Children helped with planting and harvesting, and learned about Native plants from their mothers. They spent much of their time playing—but playing with a purpose. A favorite game was shooting at targets with a

▲ A woman demonstrates how corn was made into cornmeal at a reconstructed Cherokee village in Tahlequah, Oklahoma.

Family homes belonged to ▶ women in Cherokee society and were passed down from mother to daughter.

◀ Stickball games—similar to lacrosse—remain an important part of Cherokee culture.

blowgun made from a long piece of cane. When they were ready, they would hunt squirrels and rabbits with lethal darts.

Cherokee society was matrilineal, meaning that family houses and farms belonged to the women. If a husband and wife separated, their children stayed with her. **Clan** membership—an important part of Cherokee life—was based on kinship to the mother. Clan members were regarded as brothers and sisters and were not allowed to marry. Among the most prominent clans were the Wolf Clan, Long Hair Clan, Blue Clan, Deer Clan, Paint Clan, and Wild Potato Clan. War leaders typically came from the Wolf group, while peace chiefs were from the Long Hair group. Members of the Wild Potato Clan were keepers of the land.

The potato was one of the traditional food sources that was gathered from the wild. Other plants included nuts (particularly pecans), spring onions, and blackberries. Wild turkeys were an important source of food; the Cherokees actually learned how to domesticate turkeys. They also hunted deer, elk, bears, and even bison, which grazed on the northwestern part of their territory. Cattle, pigs, and chickens arrived with Europeans, as did horses.

Games also formed a vital part of Cherokee life. Stickball games, similar to the sport of lacrosse, were the most important. All other activities came to a standstill for a stickball match. Medicine men for both sides were employed to make charms that might bring victory in the game. Frequently, the people bet all of their valuables on a game. Today, stickball is still played, both as an athletic competition and as a part of rituals at ceremonial grounds.

The Cherokees were one of the first Native American groups to have a formal written language. They also published their own newspaper, the *Cherokee Phoenix*, from 1828 to 1834.

SOMETHING SACRED

Stories are an important part of Cherokee traditional life. According to one story, long ago, the animals held a council to discuss a problem: The people were killing too many animals without showing proper respect for the lives they were taking. Each animal created an illness that would punish the people. When the plants heard what the animals were doing, they felt sorry for the people. Each plant created a cure for an illness. The story explains how the Cherokees had to learn to show respect for the lives of animals they took and to live in partnership with nature.

Another example of animals in Cherokee legends is the Water Spider. She is credited with

◀ The Water Spider plays a prominent part in Cherokee art and culture.

introducing fire to the tribe after several larger animals failed. The story teaches that no one should be dismissed because of their physical size.

In Cherokee storytelling, the world is described as a giant bowl turned upside down on a saucer, forming a big dome. The earth is underneath the dome, floating on water. The sky fills the dome all the way to the underside of the bowl, which is called the Sky Vault. The sun travels across the sky each day just beneath the Sky Vault, which is made of rock. At the end of its journey, it slips underneath the Sky Vault to return to its starting point and cross the sky again the next day.

On top of the Sky Vault is another earth-like world. The souls of departed Cherokees live there, along with spirit beings. There is also a Cherokee **underworld**. It is

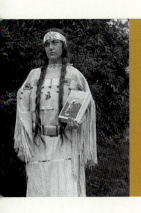

Ruth Muskrat Bronson was a young Cherokee poet who met with U.S. President Calvin Coolidge in 1923. She so impressed Coolidge during the meeting that he moved forward with a bill that granted all Native Americans citizenship. Bronson became a passionate **advocate** for the health, welfare, and education of Indigenous people.

◀ The hit Broadway musical *Oklahoma!* was inspired by the work of Lynn Riggs.

home to many powerful, dangerous spirit forces. The Cherokee people believed they lived between these worlds; many of their traditional rituals are aimed at maintaining balance and harmony between the two.

Time and again, the Cherokee storytelling tradition has found its way into American culture. Lynn Riggs was born in 1899 to a mother of Cherokee descent. Among his many stories, poems, and plays about life in Oklahoma was *Green Grow the Lilacs*. It later became a groundbreaking Broadway musical: *Oklahoma!* More recently, Brandon Hobson has become an award-winning novelist. He was a finalist for the National Book Award in 2018 and, in 2022, was awarded a Guggenheim Fellowship—a high honor reserved for people with exceptional talent in the arts.

America Meredith is both an author and artist, as well as editor of *First American Art* magazine, which celebrates the creative talents of all Native Americans. Meredith is descended from a family that includes the first Principal Chief of the Cherokee Nation, as well as perhaps the most entertaining storyteller in American history, Will Rogers. Rogers was born a citizen of the Cherokee Nation in 1879.

Will Rogers was America's most beloved actor and storyteller in the early 20th century.

PAST, PRESENT, FUTURE

Not all Cherokees marched to Oklahoma on the Trail of Tears. Some hid from federal troops. Others moved to land in Tennessee, Georgia, and Alabama. Some stayed in the Great Smoky Mountains and became North Carolina citizens. Eventually, many of these individuals regrouped to become the Eastern Band of Cherokee Indians—a federally recognized tribe based in western North Carolina.

Their reservation has a long and complicated history. It is located on the Qualla Boundary, a large tract of land that was purchased for the tribe by the white

◀ This Cherokee Nation flag celebrates the tribe's first constitution, in 1839.

A sign welcomes visitors to the Qualla Boundary in Western North Carolina.

adopted son of a Cherokee chief. It was taken over by the U.S. government—and then sold back to the Cherokees.

Today, the Eastern Band is focused on preserving the Cherokee language, as well as protecting the archaeological sites of the Cherokees' mound-building ancestors. More than 15,000 people are members of the Eastern Band, with almost two-thirds living on or near reservation land. A hotel and casino on the reservation has been extremely successful. It has helped to fund a new school and hospital and public housing.

The Cherokee Nation headquarters complex is located in Tahlequah, Oklahoma.

Two federally recognized Cherokee tribes are headquartered in the northeastern Oklahoma town of Tahlequah: the United Keetoowah Band of Cherokee Indians and the Cherokee Nation. Both are also dedicated to preserving the Cherokee language. Like the Eastern Band, they have created **language immersion** programs in the school systems they operate.

The Cherokee Nation is the largest Native American tribe in the United States, with more than

◀ One way the Cherokees keep their culture alive is through ceremonial gatherings and celebrations. This man captures the tribe's warrior tradition.

450,000 members. Around 140,000 live on the Oklahoma reservation. The tribe employs more than 11,000 people in the businesses it runs. These businesses include healthcare, education, construction, **infrastructure** development, and environmental protection. The federal government used to oversee many of these activities, but returned them to Cherokee control. The Cherokees have demonstrated a superb talent for organization and self-government dating back more than 200 years, which continues to this day.

◀ Dennis Wolfe, a Cherokee leader in the 1970s and 1980s, was one of many people who helped preserve the tribe's language and culture.

Each September, over Labor Day weekend, more than 150,000 people gather in Tahlequah for the Cherokee National Holiday festival. It celebrates the shared history and culture of the Cherokee people and includes an **intertribal powwow** where dancers compete for prizes. There are also stickball and blowgun competitions and a parade featuring traditional costumes. The early September date was selected to honor the creation of the first Cherokee Nation Constitution, on September 6, 1839.

GLOSSARY AND FURTHER READING

GLOSSARY

Advocate—Someone who supports a cause.

Clan—A close-knit extended family related by kinship or common ancestors.

Coveted—Greatly desired.

Disfiguring—Spoiling the appearance of a person.

Domes—Large rock formations with sides that slope down from a central high point.

Ecosystem—A group of living and non-living things that create nutrients and energy within an area.

Ethnic Cleansing—The mass removal (or killing) of members of an unwanted group of people, typically on racial grounds.

Federal—Related to the national government.

French and Indian War—A conflict over control of North America from 1754 to 1763 between France and England. French soldiers and their Native American allies fought against British forces, including American colonists and their Native American allies.

Frontier—The imaginary line that marks the edge of a group's territory.

Infrastructure—The organization of roads, buildings, and supplies that support a society.

Intertribal Powwow—A large Native American ceremony or celebration that includes different tribes.

Language Immersion—A method of teaching the vocabulary and grammar of a language.

Plantations—Large farming or agricultural operations.

Resettlement—The transfer of a large group of people from one place to another.

Resilience— The ability to recover quickly from difficulties.

Smallpox— A virus brought to the Americas by Europeans, for which Indigenous people had no natural immunity. By the mid-1800s, more than 75 percent of Native Americans may have died of the disease.

Smelting—The process of extracting metals contained ion rocks.

Turbans—Headwear created by wrapping a length of cloth around the head.

Underworld—An imaginary place, usually below the earth, where departed souls go.

BOOKS

Krupat, Arnold. *Boarding School Voices: Carlisle Indian School Students Speak.* Lincoln, NE: University of Nebraska Press, 2021.

Rossiter, Brienna. *The Trail of Tears.* Mendota Heights, MN: North Star Editions, 2025.

Tyler, Ron. *Native Americans: The Complete Plates of McKenney, Catlin, and Bodmer.* Cologne, Germany: Taschen America, 2024.

Various Authors. *My Life: Growing Up Native in America.* New York, NY: MTV Books/Simon & Schuster Children's Publishing, 2024.

ABOUT THE AUTHOR

MARK STEWART has written more than 150 nonfiction books for educational publishers, covering history, sports, and popular culture. His family tree tells a complex story common to many Americans. Mark's ancestors include some of the first European colonists, as well as the Indigenous people with whom early settlers interacted. Some faced off on the field of battle while others fought side-by-side. His 10th great-grandfather was **Myles Standish**, an officer on the *Mayflower*, while his ninth great-grandmother was **Singing Bird Corbison**, who was described as a "Shawnee woman" but who was probably from the **Wampanoag** tribe. The Wampanoag people saved Standish and his fellow **Pilgrims** from starvation during the winter of 1620–21, forming the basis for the story of Thanksgiving. The descendants of Corbison and Standish blended into a single family in 1789, and then headed west in search of opportunity. This brought Mark's ancestors into direct conflict with Native people along the frontier in the 1700s and 1800s. Mark's sixth great-grandmother recalled frantically casting bullets for her husband as they defended their small Kentucky fort from an attack. Another served under 23-year-old **Abraham Lincoln** in the Illinois Militia during the Black Hawk War of 1832. Mark's more recent ancestors chose to fight their battles with words—as writers and editors of books, newspapers and magazines. In 2007, he authored a history of the **Indian Removal Act of 1830** and the infamous **Trail of Tears**.

INDEX

B
Boone, Daniel 6, 11
Boone, Jemimah 11
Bowie, Jim 13
Bronson, Ruth Muskrat. 21

C
Carlisle Indian School. 15
Cherokee National Holiday 29
Cherokee Phoenix 19
Coolidge, Calvin 21
Cooper, James Fenimore 11
Creek 8, 9, 13, 14
Cumberland Gap 6

D
De Soto, Hernan 8

H
Hobson, Brandon. 22

I
Indian Removal Act 14

J
Jackson, Andrew 13, 14

M
Meredith, America 23

O
Oconostota 10
Oklahoma! 22

Q
Qualla Boundary 24, 25

R
Riggs, Lynn. 22
Rogers, Will 23

T
Trail of Tears. 7, 15, 24
Treaty of New Echota. 15

W
Water Spider 20
Wolfe, Dennis. 28